NAT
in word

written & illustrated b

adapted by

LONDON •

First published in 1979
by Editions Gallimard, Paris
First published in Great Britain
in 1980 by
Chatto & Windus Ltd.
40 William IV Street
London WC2N 4DF
Text and illustrations © 1979 Colette Portal
English translation © 1980 Chatto & Windus
ISBN 0 7011 2515 2
All rights reserved
Printed and bound in Italy

URE ALIVE
s and pictures

COLETTE PORTAL

Madeleine and D. J. Enright

CHATTO AND WINDUS • 1980

Contents
The Poppy	*page* 6
The Mushroom	10
Wheat and Bread	14
Underground Granaries	18
The Messenger Bee	22
The Maybugs	26
The Frogs	30
Volcanoes	34
Clouds	38
The Moon	42

The Poppy

1. Each spring a flower rises, simple, vivid and fragile. It fades as soon as plucked. From bud to seed, here is the story of the poppy of the fields.

2. One morning, on the tip of its stem a bud shows itself, takes shape, and grows. It is ready to open. Head bent towards the earth, as if for a last look at its origin, it straightens up at the very moment of its blossoming.

3. The dawn witnesses thousands of these quiet births. The two sepals open and reveal the still captive flower. For the first time light penetrates into the pleated chamber, with its little patch of red.

4. Caressed by the light, warmed by the silent rays of the sun, the flower swells. The sepals part. Freed, the four petals, coiled and creased, still retain the shape of the bud.

5. The bud becomes a corolla. The petals open. A pistil rises, circled with stamens. The pistil is female, the stamens male.

6. The wind and the winged creatures passing by work together to create countless seeds. Each seed becomes a poppy. The corolla unfolds. The petals uncrease.

7. With the dry heat a fine dust of pollen escapes from the stamens. The poppy's pollen is sometimes the colour of verdigris, sometimes yellowish, orange, red or crimson. If you brush against it with your fingers, it leaves hardly a trace on them. At the least breath of air, it flies away towards other open corollas.

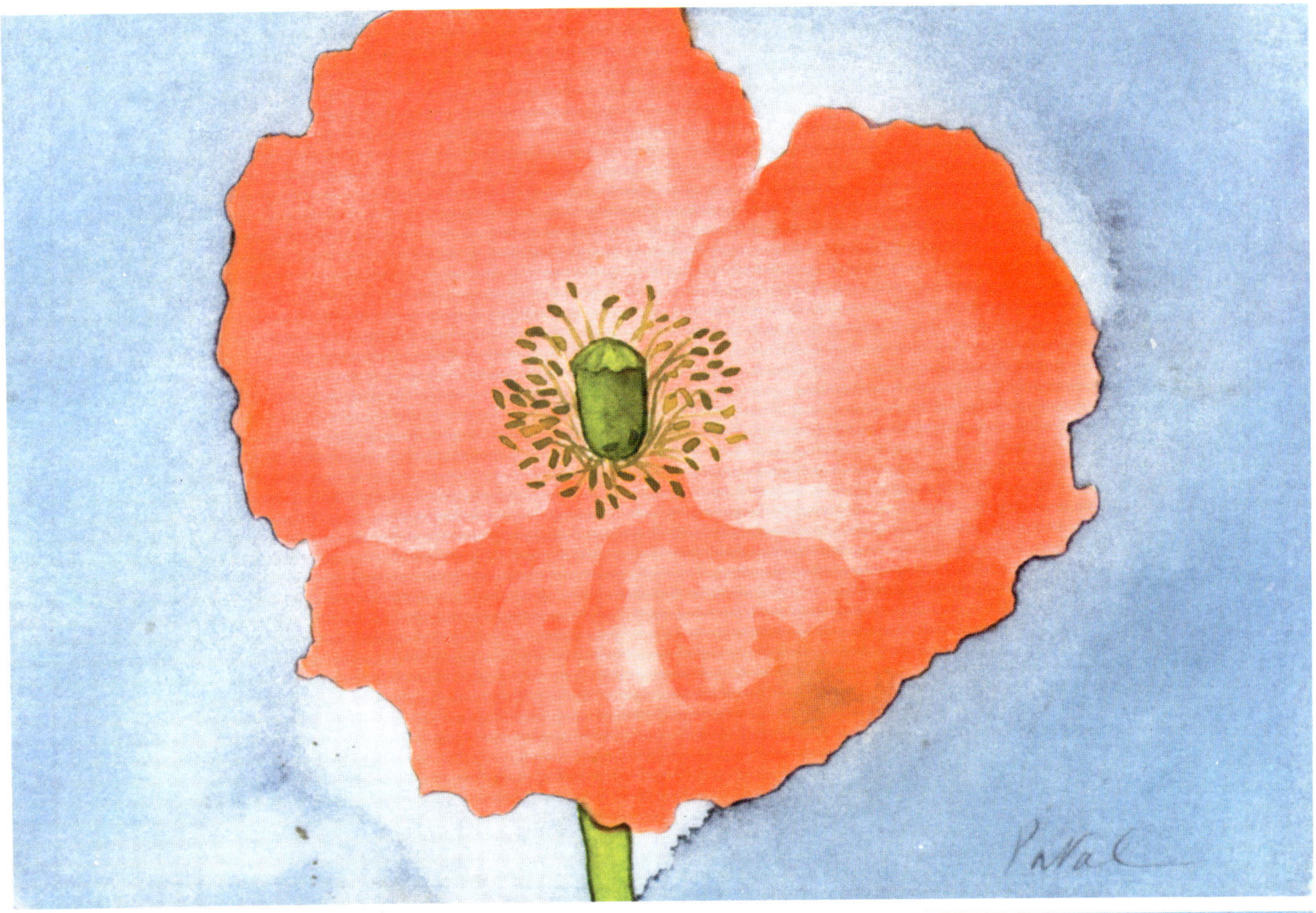

5
6 | 8
7

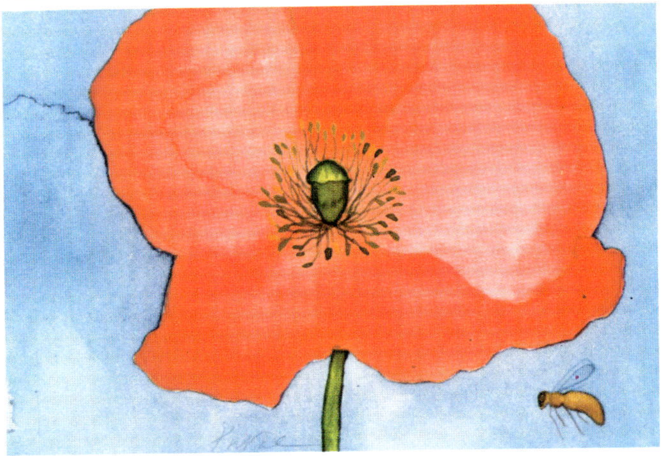

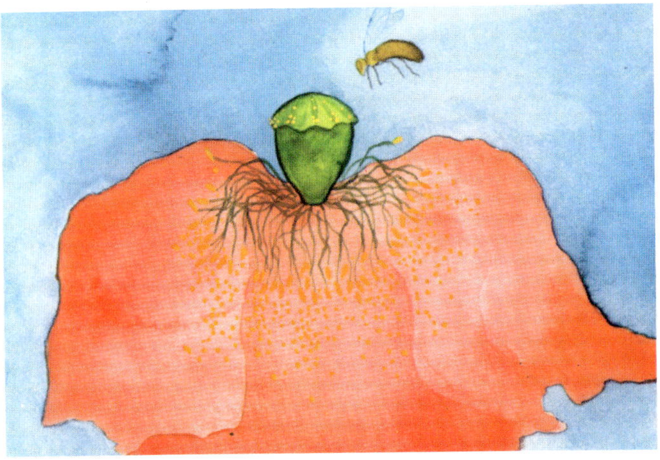

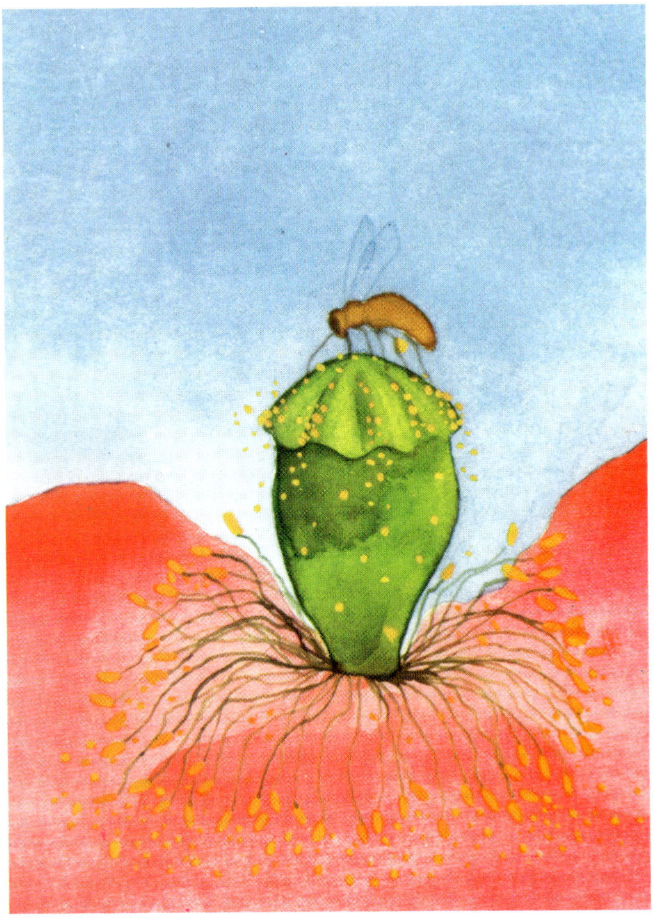

8. The pollen, this intangible dust, has the power of giving life. Abandoned to the whims of the wind, to the coming and going of insects, the pollen rains on the stigmas radiating above the pistil. Long and slim papillas, coated with a sweet juice, capture it. Pollination is achieved.

9. The pollen fallen on the petals is wasted. The pollen retained by the stigmas sinks into the pistil, then reaches an ovule. Their substances mix, and the ovule has found its chance of becoming a seed.

10. The flower has been fertilised. Stamens and faded petals fall. The pistil alone, filled with life, changes into a fruit. The ovules change into seeds.

11. The fruit is ripe. The roof of the pistil lifts, opens. The enclosed seeds, until now hidden and sheltered, fall one by one, as the currents of air carry them.

12. During the autumn days thousands of seeds, scattered by the wind, mix with the earth. Strengthened by sleep and oblivion, they will spend the winter unseen, hidden in the darkness of the underground world, protected against cold and frost. This is a time of silence.

13. Winter passes. The earth, hardened by the cold, grows warmer every day. On the surface of the ground a new life stirs. The fields become green again. The vigorous young seed, with its long roots, white and tender, hooks itself on every clod of earth, on every pebble. It begins its perilous adventure against all obstacles, using the obstacles as supports.

14. A pale, green, wavering stem rises and rises. One leaf to the left, one leaf to the right. At the tip of the stem, a bud appears and takes shape. Another stem, other leaves, other buds. With the help of the sun, the goddess Demeter, goddess of fertility, carries out her task. The poppy's future is secure.

The Mushroom

1. It is still raining, but it is pleasant to walk along the forest paths. Autumn has arrived with September. Under the debris of broken twigs, under the rotten leaves, in the mould, a pale white button grows: the ghost of the vegetable kingdom.

2. In the depths of the dark forest, innumerable noises of walking, of crawling. In the wet meadows, through the rustling of leaves, the sound of birds taking wing.

3. The ghost of the vegetable world, so clean, so white, so well wrapped in its veil, grows on its stem and shows its cap. The field agaric finds its life in what is dead.

4. The stem grows, pushing up the cap...

5. It pushes so much that cap and stem part. A few days later, a ring, vestige of the veil, remains attached to the stem, the only trace of their union.

6. Under the umbrella-cap – for it is still raining – pink blades in profusion radiate above the stem, a

fine dust of spores escaping from them, thousands of spores.

7. At the least breath of air they escape and fall in a circle on the ground.

8. The mushroom of the woods, friend of uncertain shadows, stranger to all that shines, has given its seed to the earth, and the earth returns it a hundredfold. In secret, quite invisible, the spores sink into the leaf-mould, the rich rotten substance of the soil.

9. At times the sun darts through the branches and, warmed up, the soil steams. But every day the rain, boring, annoying rain, enriches the soil. The rain is a blessing from the sky. Rain and dew form part of the world's harmony.

10. The soil is moist, the earth is warm. It is the right time for a spore to germinate. Very quickly, fine filaments spread in all directions, growing, spinning a subterranean network: the thread-like spawn. On the surface of the soil, little round white dots appear in a circle, a 'fairy ring'.

11. A crow caws and the leaves fall.

12. Small round white dots, in a 'fairy ring', friends of the shade, strangers to the light, grow...

13–15. ... grow, under the trees, after the rain.

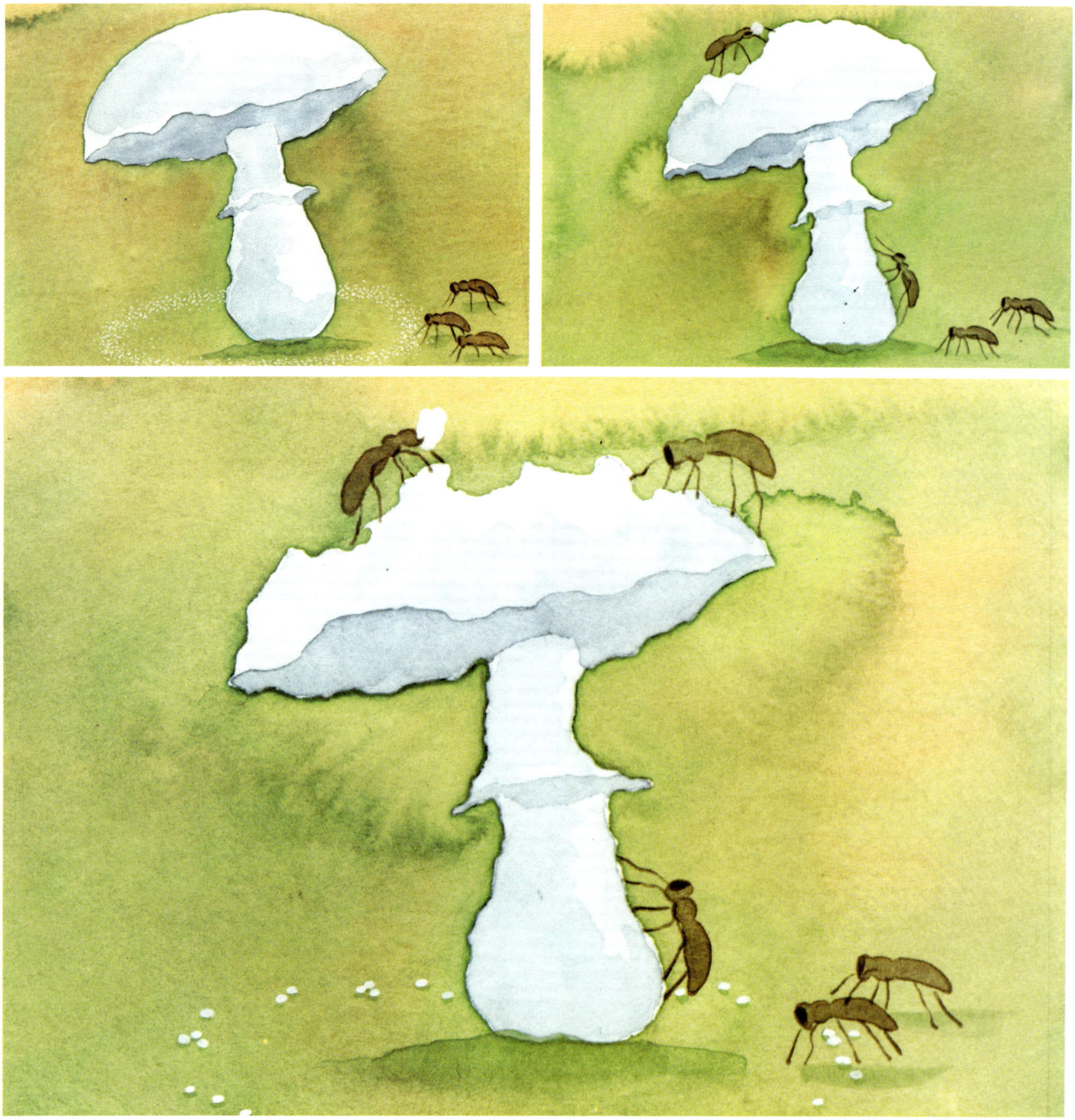

Wheat and Bread

1. The earth, which alone gives birth and food to all creatures, receives the fertile seed. A grain of wheat, the most beautiful of earth's fruits, is the promise of thousands of ears of wheat.

2. Between October and November a grain of wheat is sown in well prepared soil. The harrow breaks the clods, the roller firms them in depth. The bed is ready for the seeds. The earth is not yet cold, just damp enough for the seed to germinate. The cycle of germination begins.

3. Three roots. The first blade breaks the surface of the earth. It unfolds and the tip of the second one appears wrapped in its protective envelope. Between these two, the tip of a third one. Then five roots.

4. The rhizome, finer than the stalk, forms just below the surface of the ground. Emptied of its substance, the seed dries up while the roots lengthen. The stalk grows, rises, and the thallus, the body of the plant, thickens at its base. Then other stalks form, from which other leaves sprout. A chill runs through the earth. Everything comes to a halt.

5. December: all the way to the horizon, winter wheat has risen. But the cold stops all growth. The nights are long, the dawns tardy.

6. One morning the fields are white. Breaking the silence, the crows search for grain that has failed to germinate.

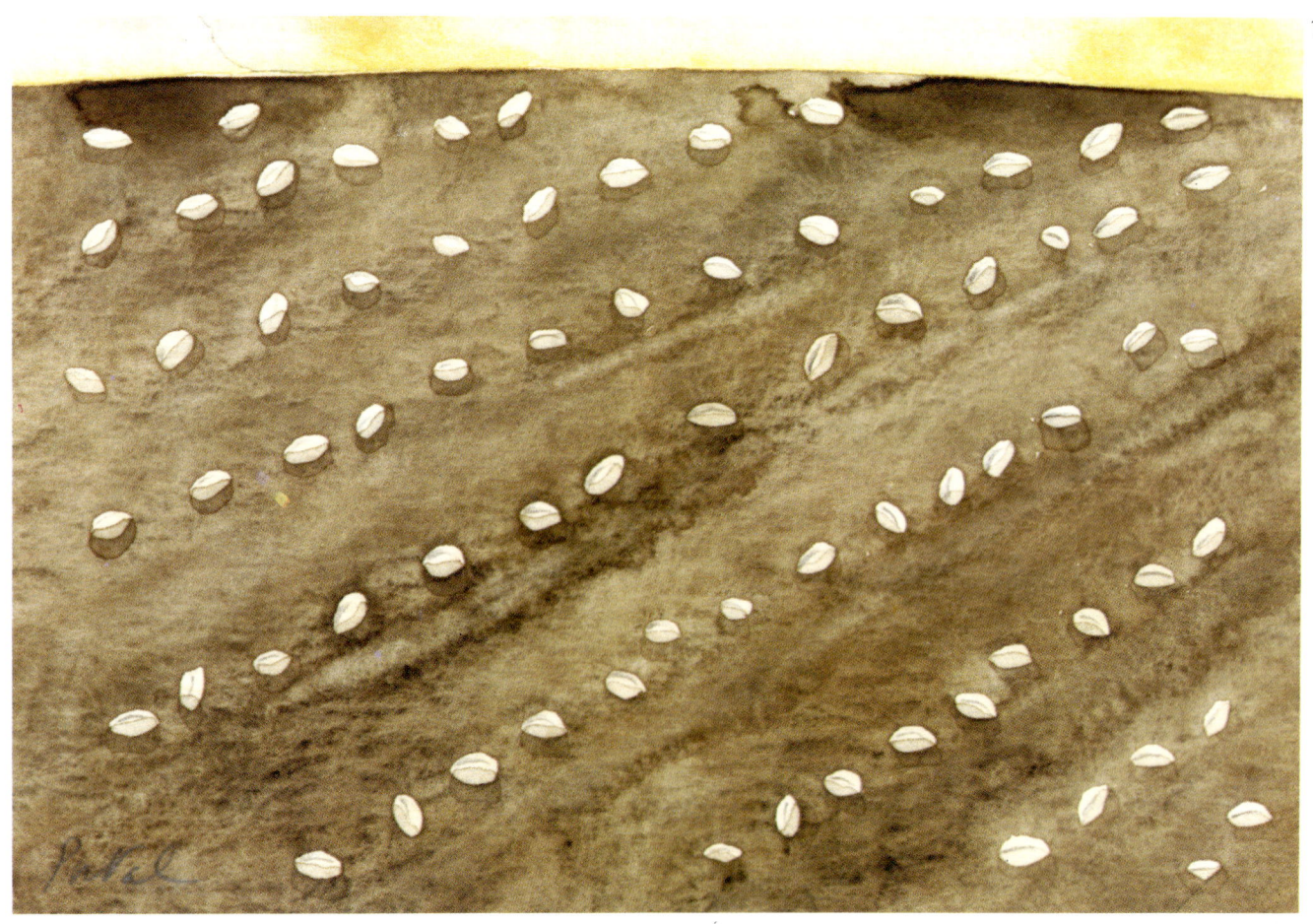

7. Spring: everything is soft and tender, the air, the smells, the sounds. The stalks pursue their growth. From each of them, two leaves. Between the leaves, the terminal bud that will give the main ear of wheat. If there are many stalks there will be many ears.

8. At the tip of the stalks the small ears swing in the wind. They flower. The ear of wheat reaches its fullness. It bends slightly, heavy with so many grains, wheat grains, tomorrow's bread.

9. During the long summer days the fields undulate and tremble like a sea, reaching to the horizon. It is harvest time. The combine harvester separates the grain from the straw. The grain to feed on, the straw to sleep on.

10. Later, in the autumn, the stubble is burnt.

11. Before the nimble harvest rat can get at them, the tractor takes the ears to the farm. The grain is sorted out, the wheat separated from the tares, the

15

broken seeds, the soil, the insects dead or alive. The clean grain is dried and stored away from the cold and the wet, from birds and predators, from parasites and diseases.

12. The origin of wheat is unknown. But its history is closely linked with man's.

From Mesopotamia to Egypt, from India to China, it was universally grown, and still is nowadays.

The wheat, so hard when taken out of the soil, becomes this light white powder: flour.

13–14. In a bowl, put 1kg. (2lb.) flour, 30g. (1oz.) baker's yeast dissolved in 375ml. (1pt.) warm water, a little salt, a dash of olive oil. Mix well, and work, and knead, and knead, and work, and mix. Therein lies the secret of a good loaf. Let it rest for half an hour. Put it in a hot oven for fifty minutes. Here is bread, your bread.

Underground Granaries

1. An amorous frenzy reigns among the ants: the nuptial flight is nearing. At the end of a warm afternoon the winged ants swirl upwards. Like a living cloud ceaselessly changing its shape, they reach a considerable height. Then, all at once, they pair off.

2. On the ground the males impregnate the queens. Having accomplished their function, they die. The female, heavy with the promise of the future, big with the royal seed, will go and found new empires.

3. She looks for a hiding place, a crack in the earth, a hole. In the shade of a pebble, she digs a nest and quickly plugs the entrance to her self-imposed prison. Destined to remain underground, she tears off her nuptial wings, now useless.

4. She digs the first gallery and at once lays her first eggs there. Each egg becomes a larva, blind and limbless. Each larva becomes a pupa wrapped in a cocoon, each pupa an ant.

5. Eggs, larvae, cocoons, they are the object of tireless care. The first worker ants are born. Fragile and transparent, they set to work at once. They will be architects, nannies, harvesters, guards, thieves and brigands too.

6. The young worker ant is watchful. She joins in the communal life without any apprenticeship, lending a leg with the business of the nest, in charge of the catering for the whole community. She climbs the gallery, hoists herself up, bustling and jostling. With enough strength to lift a mountain, she pushes away at the pebble closing

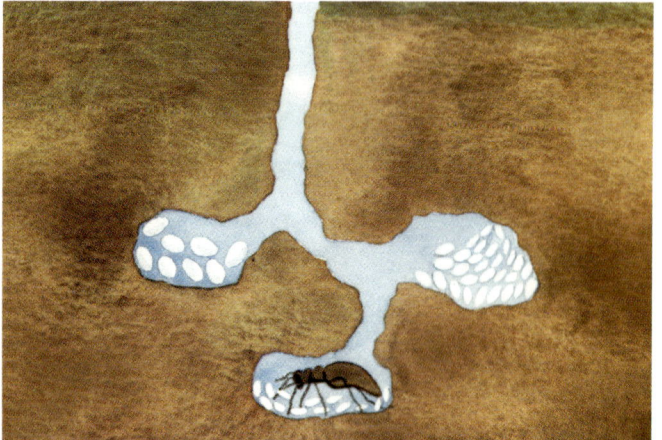

her prison. The worker ant will know the blessing of the sun on her back, a blessing the Queen will never enjoy again.

7. A file of ants sets out in search of food. Pulse or chickweed, butterflies' wings, wild clover seed, a grain of corn or a poppy.

8. The ant rubs her antennae together and pats her neighbour's. An exchange of smells or of caresses, these pattings are the means of communication across the whole colony. The ants exchange fragments of food. Their jaws are their defensive weapons, their scissors to cut, their tools to crush and pound, to snap and break, and tear and peel, the instruments they use to lift, carry and pull.

9. The crop is rich. Loaded with their harvest, the ants march in procession along the ant-trails.

10. In the life they lead close to the earth, the worker ants need most of all the senses of smell, taste and touch, the three senses linked to the

antennae. Despite their bright black eyes, sight is only secondary for them.

11. They return to the ant-hill, their smell marking the trail. From mandible to mandible, from leg to leg, wheat grains, maize, poppies, are passed down into the depths of the enormous underground belly.

12. In the centre of a deep labyrinth of vaults, tunnels, galleries and granaries, the ant puts away the food for the coming year. The Queen, always busy, lays her eggs.

13. When the north wind returns, there is nothing left, not the tiniest morsel of fly or grain, not the tiniest morsel of anything. A pebble protects the entrance to the ant-hill from winter's many dangers.

14. Above the ground, a pebble conceals a kingdom.

The Messenger Bee

1. The sun rises on the cold meadows. In a patch of sunlight a bee-keeper has placed a rough wooden box: a bee-hive, an empire of sleep. For millions of years, every morning, a honey-gatherer has left the hive in search of the daily pollen.

2. Over fields and gardens she flies, looking for the flower that will yield its harvest. Hers is no idle life, she flies here and there all over the yet unexplored countryside.

3. A source is found. Petals and corollas, stamens and pistils. The trembling container, the flower, is open to the looter. Skilled in the confusion of the flower's heart, she alights and gathers.

4. Nectar coats her hairs and wings. The pollen clings to her legs, she is loaded to the limit of her strength.

5. The wings, with their leaf-like veins, beat. The hive is close by.

6. Heavy with her treasure, the provider comes back to unload her booty and inform her companions of the lucky find.

7. She enters the silent temple. Honeycombs, cakes of wax, impregnable but fragile. The light does not reach the cells. Builders of model cities, the bees care nothing for the incidental beauty they have created. In the silence, the noise of wings.

8. The messenger bee settles on the honeycomb, at once surrounded by her companions. To each one she offers the nectar and the pollen she has discovered.

9. In a figure of eight, she first traces a short straight line and then commences a quivering dance. She comes back to her point of departure in a semi-circle. Another quivering dance, another semi-circle, but on the other side. The straight line points towards the source. The gatherers join in the dance, following the messenger.

10. Message received, the gatherers leave the hive and find the flower without fail: at a distance of a hundred yards.

11. One flower, one bee. A hundred flowers, a hundred bees.

Myriads of faceted eyes reflect this riot of colour. The bees plunge into the flowers, shoving one another, scraping the pollen with their mandibles, gathering it with their hind-feet and piling it in small hollows in their legs. If you pause nearby, you can hear the buzzing of the looters.

12. Along their legs, in the hollow baskets, the pollen piles up. Small balls of lavender, of marjoram, of rosemary. The summer flowers are beautiful, the bees are rich.

Over the fields, through streams of perfume, they return to the hive.

13. Each cell receives its ration of precious pollen. The bees are careful not to mix lavender pollen with rosemary pollen or any other pollen of the meadows.

14. From hive to flowers, from flowers to hive, until dusk, until the light fades.

This is the meaning of the dance of the flowers, floating between earth and sky.

11
12
13 14

The Maybugs

1. In June, near the surface of the ground, seventy eggs laid in small stacks will hatch in a hole dug a month before.

2. At the end of July each egg becomes a larva, or grub. The grub is small, with a ringed body, no wings, a tough brown head. It is hungry, it eats the roots and grows fat. Its skin bursts, rips, drops. The grub has cast its skin.

3. With the first cold days of September, when chilly mists cover the earth, when the sly north wind sneaks between furrows and clods, the grub sinks deep, deeper into the ground. It does not take any food, it slows down the rhythm of its life.

4. With the next spring, the second, the grub comes up to the surface and starts an active life. It devours small roots, devours big roots, and grows. The skin bursts, a second transformation has taken place. One morning the gardener is worried: there are holes in the carrots. The enemy is in the garden, and the hunt for the grub is on.

5. During the second winter, the grub, numb with cold, digs itself in deeper.

6. By the third spring it has become a fat white worm. It devours the carrots and the turnips, and the roots of the trees, the tender young roots and the tough old ones. In the garden, ruin and waste; the gardener is in despair.

7. During the third autumn, the grub surrounds itself with a thick hard skin inside a shell made of earth mixed with spittle. It is a pupa, a motionless shape.

8. In solitude and darkness, an extraordinary transformation occurs inside its skin. Everything becomes shapeless pulp. Then wings, legs, a head; a complete maybug has taken shape. An adult, a perfect insect. The metamorphosis has taken three years.

9. Numb all through the winter in its pupa wrapping, the maybug starts its slow ascension towards the surface of the ground. It is May.

10. On the evening of a warm day, with its insect strength it pushes the earth aside. For the first time it sees daylight.

11. Under the brown elytrons, the wing-case, the quivering wings unfold. The maybug flies to the nearest tree.

12. A deep buzzing sound is heard. The maybugs are chopping away at the leaves of the plum-trees

in the orchard, of the oak-trees in the forest. Havoc prevails.

13. Light fades away, the air is still warm and the maybugs mate. After three years in darkness, they live for three luminous weeks.

14. Before dying, the female digs a little hole in the ground in which she lays her eggs in small stacks. They will soon hatch. In three years, it wil be maybug time.

The Frogs

1–2. On the river-bank a green frog has laid its spawn. Abandoned among the reeds, five thousand black dots held in a transparent cluster await their metamorphosis.

3. Five thousand embryos stir, unfold, lengthen. Then, gently warmed by the May sun, they hatch and come out of their envelope, clinging to the shell.

4. This creature, so unlike a frog, without legs or mouth, but with a head and a tail, breathes through gills and swims well and fast. It is a tadpole, a hungry tadpole, it eats algae.

5. The tadpole grows. It has two legs. Its tail looks as fragile as a veil, but its appearance is deceptive. In search of food it moves with frantic energy.

6. The tadpole has four legs. It comes and breathes at the surface of the water. Its gills, now useless, disappear. Its agitated movements disturb the peaceful water. Tadpoles in their thousands swarm in lakes and pools and ponds.

7. With a remnant of a tail, the only evidence of its life in the water, the green frog leaves the silence of the pools.

8. The tail has gone. The frog is squat, its skin cold and bare, without hair, feathers or scales. It slips from your hands if you try to hold it. The green frog is three months old. Its metamorphosis is complete. Batrachian, amphibious, swimmer and jumper, carnivore and singer, it begins its existence on land.

5
6
7

9. The motionless waters are a mirror for the passing insect.

10. Dragonfly, bee, butterfly, fly and mosquito are all easy prey. Two large yellow eyes follow these innocents when they come too close to the mirror in their graceful and short-lived dance.

11. Suddenly, without warning, the frog jumps. Quick as lightning, with a dry clicking noise, its tongue traps the insect.

12. The frog plunges at once, carrying its victim to its solitary hiding place. Listen to the sound of the water.

13. One evening in May the frogs fall in love. By the water's edge males and females gather. A strange sound troubles the dusk. It is the voice of the male calling to the female.

14. Curious little bags swell on each side of his throat. It is the croak-box, the song of the pond. It lasts two or three seconds, stops, and starts again. This din will go on, night and day.

15. The male chooses his mate. They leave the crowd for a secluded place. He climbs on her back, then they jump into the water, inseparably joined. The male spills his seed on the eggs laid by the female.

Fertilised, they float in clusters just below the surface of the water, among the reeds.

Volcanoes

1-10. On the 5th of February, A.D. 62, a clear winter's day, a slight tremor shook the city of Pompeii and its neighbourhood, its inhabitants and their emperor Nero. Temples, arches and statues swayed. Seventeen years later, in the summer of 79, Vesuvius burst its sides and vomited fire from the earth.

In the third century A.D., the writer Dio Cassius described the beginning of the eruption as follows:

'The rumblings were growing more frequent, some sounding like underground thunder, others, on the surface, like the roaring of beasts; the noise of the sea added to the din, echoed by the sky. Suddenly came a formidable tearing; enormous rocks were flung outwards. An immense fire rose, a thick smoke darkened the air and the sun was hidden as during an eclipse. Day became night, light became darkness. Some believed that the Giants had rebelled again, others that the whole universe was disintegrating, returning to chaos and fire. They fled through the streets, from land to sea, from sea to land, for in their terror they thought anywhere was safer than the place where they happened to be. An incredible mass of ashes covered the sea as well as the land, filling the whole atmosphere. It caused great damage, ruining the fields, killing men and beasts, and all the birds, and all the fish. It buried two whole cities, Herculaneum and Pompeii. There was so much dust that some of it reached Africa, Egypt, Syria and Rome. It caused an immense panic for several days, for whether or not they had witnessed the cataclysm, people believed that the whole world had gone into convulsions, that the sun was going

to disappear, swallowed up by the earth, and that the earth would be lifted up into the sky.'

11. A volcano consists of three parts: a chimney leading from the depths of the earth to the surface, the molten magma, and the mountain, which is a crater, a cone, a dome or a solidified lava flow. The vulcanian type: Vulcano (Lipari Islands) is a famous example of spectacular eruptions of this type. The viscous lava blocks the chimney; then, impelled by the gases, the compressed magma explodes violently. The lava foam, pulverised, falls back in thousands of cinders: pumice stones. An immense black plume rises, and comes down again in a rain of ashes, covering everything and suffocating all life.

12. *The pelean type:* Mount Pelée in Martinique gave its name to this type of volcano. Very thick and viscous lava obstructs the chimney and forms a dome. Under the pressure of the gases, the dome cracks, giving vent to an enormous cloud of steam and burning ashes. These fiery clouds roll down

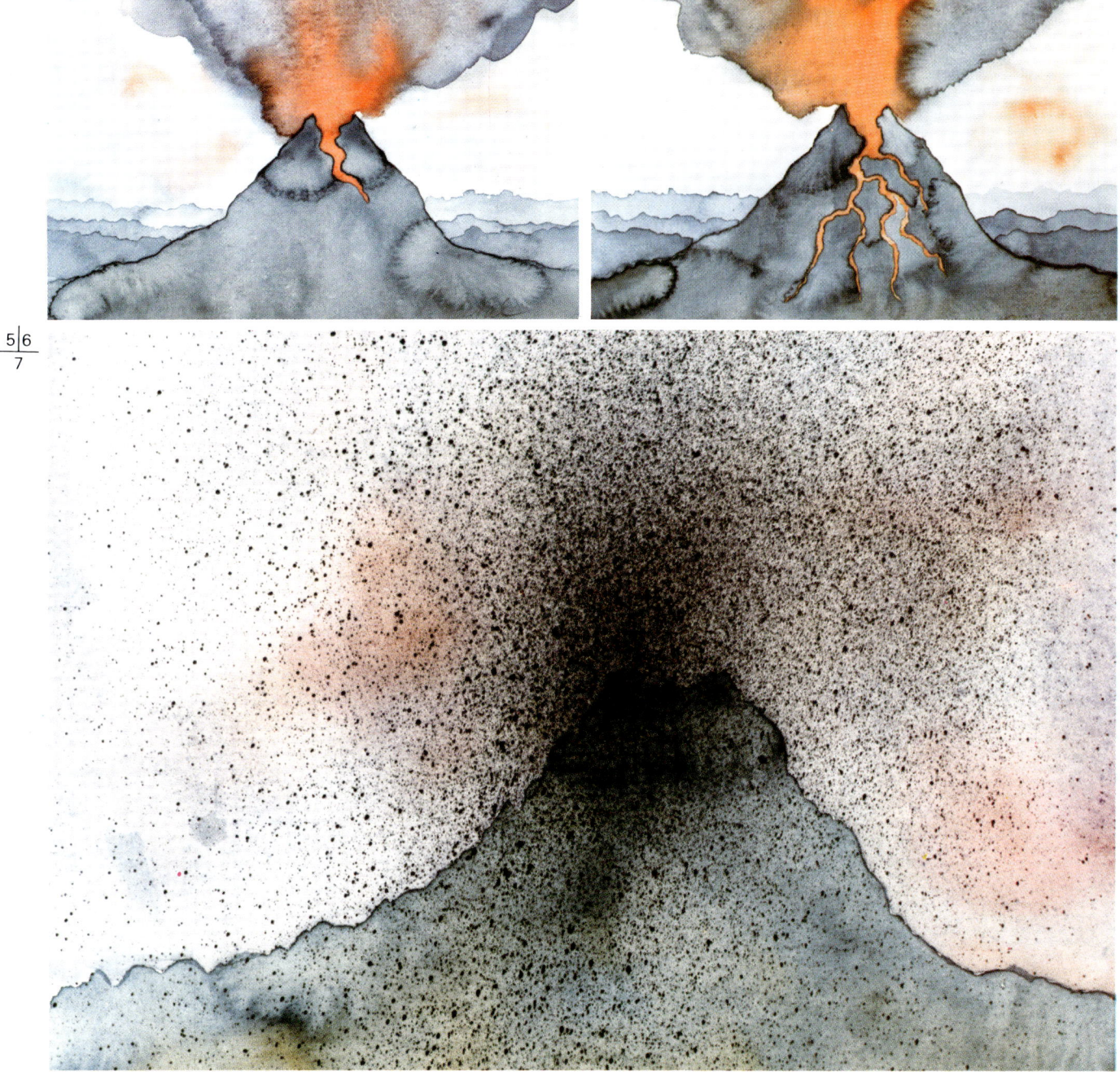

the slopes of the mountain, crushing, suffocating and burning.

13. *The Hawaian type:* Mauna Loa is a volcano of this type. Layer on layer of fluid lava have formed a low and gaping cone. Inside the immense crater, the lava boils ceaselessly at a temperature of twelve hundred degrees centigrade. At the moment of eruption it overflows and streams down the slopes, rushing through the plains in rivers of fire and scorching everything in its passage.

14. *The Strombolian type:* Stromboli, the 'lighthouse of the Mediterranean', has for centuries vomited volcanic bombs and thick sticky lava through a large gash torn in its crater.

Volcanic eruptions usually occur after a long sleep. Then memories die out: vegetation grows anew and life, stronger than death, again clothes the vast expanses of scorched earth with greenness.

Clouds

Intangible and elusive, the cloud seems to float, in spite of the huge mass of fine water droplets it carries.

1. *Cirrus:* it is the highest of all clouds, ten thousand metres (30,000 feet) high, and sometimes more. It is a frozen cloud and has the appearance of delicate filaments: 'mare's-tails'. It does not bring rain.

2. *Cirro-stratus:* less high than the cirrus, between six and ten thousand metres (20,000-30,000 feet). A thin whitish veil, it is made of minute ice crystals. It is so thin that it does not dim the brilliance of the sun. A wonderful optical phenomenon occurs: a halo in the colours of the rainbow. The cirro-stratus heralds rain.

3. *Alto-stratus:* it often follows the cirro-stratus whose mass has thickened and descended. Between two and six thousand metres (6,000-20,000 feet). A heavier and darker veil, producing an overcast sky. But it is not thick enough to hide the sun. It is formed of fine droplets at its base and ice crystals higher up. The ice crystals falling on the droplets turn into rain.

4. *Nimbo-stratus:* its altitude is two thousand metres (6,000 feet). It forms a dark grey layer completely veiling the sun. It brings heavy rain.

5. *The rainbow:* symbol of communication between heaven and earth, it is the floating bridge of the sky. Violet, indigo, blue, green, yellow, orange and red. In the past, pagans saw in it the scarf of Iris, messenger of the gods.

1	2
3	4

6. *Stratus:* it is the lowest of all clouds, and the most uniform. Its altitude is less than two thousand five hundred metres (8,000 feet). Low, grey, flat cloud, it closes off the horizon, hides the furrows of the fields, penetrates walls with its humidity. It is the cloud of the cold season and grey days; it is fog.

7. *Mist:* no wind on the surface of the earth, and no wind higher up. The air settles near the ground, forming layers of mist. Morning mist, evening mist, the mist and drizzle of the sea-shores. If the temperature of the ground falls below zero, the early morning sees the plants covered with ice crystals: it is hoar frost. Calm night, muted sounds.

8. *Cumulus humilis:* the small cumulus of fine weather, the lonely cloud wandering in the sky. It has a sharply defined shape. It floats between two and ten thousand metres (6,000-30,000 feet). Its base is dark, its summit a vivid blue.

9. *Alto-cumulus:* the sky looks dappled, a 'mackerel sky'. Several small cumuli joined in regular

lines give it this appearance. They indicate the instability of the air.

10. *Cumulus congestus:* a thick cloud with neat contours towering up in the sky. It heralds short and violent showers.

11. *Cumulo-nimbus:* the storm-cloud, it carries lightning and thunder; it is the cloud of summer and hot days, the king of clouds.

12. *Lightning and thunder:* like the rain, they are seed, or punishment, from the heavens.

13. *Strato-cumulus:* close to the surface of the earth, it is made up of lines of cumulus clouds, like streets of clouds.

14. *Sunset:* space is bathed in quiet splendour. A poet has written of
    'The fair, frail palaces,
The fading alps and archipelagoes,
And great cloud-continents of sunset-seas.'

The Moon

For four billion and six hundred million years, the Moon, queen of the night, has been shining. Its brilliance is only the reflection of the light of the Sun. It is the guide of the nomads of the night. Waxing, waning and disappearing, it follows the rhythms of life. It is the star of eternal recurrence. While the Earth revolves around the Sun, the Moon revolves around the Earth in the same time as it rotates on itself, in twenty-nine days, twelve hours and forty-four minutes.

1. It is the night of the new Moon. When it departs from an imaginary straight line joining the Sun to the Earth, the thin crescent rises in the east.

2. Night after night the rising of the Moon is later by fifty minutes. Its shape derives from this variation. Hanging between sky and earth, the thin horned crescent grows little by little.

3. Seven days after its first appearance, the still waxing Moon has performed one quarter of its revolution and shows its first quarter. As it is setting later every day, it can be seen brighter and more luminous at its rising.

4–5. On the eleventh night, three quarters of the Moon are illuminated. It is the gibbous phase: the Moon is hunch-backed.

6. On the fifteenth night, almost at the moment when the Sun disappears, the Moon appears at its highest position, round, beautiful, resplendent; it is midnight. It is full moon. But the full Moon is only half of the Moon.

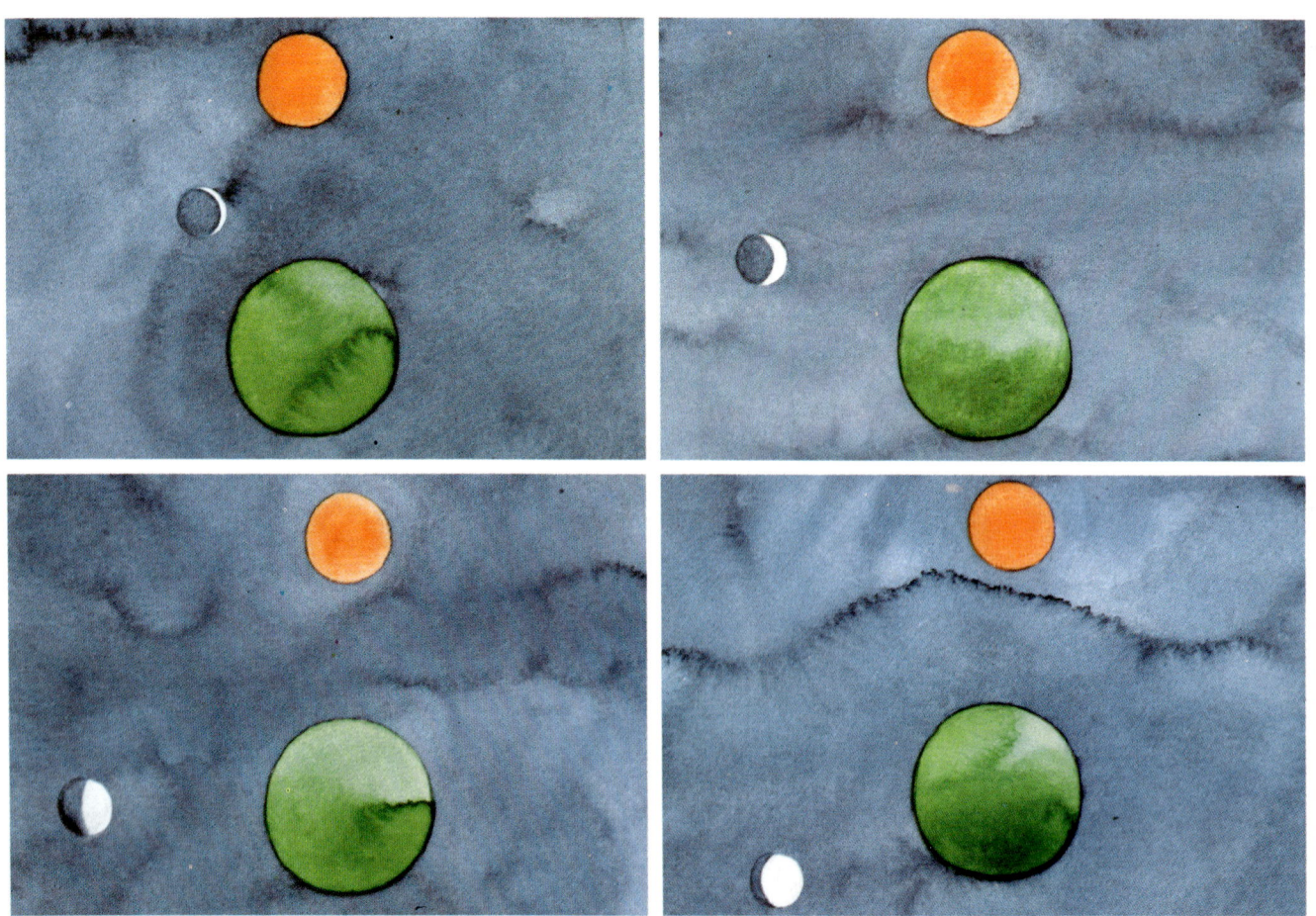

7–9. A few days afterwards, it shows up late in the night. Waning, it repeats in reverse the phases it has just been through. It performs its revolution around the Earth at the same time as its slow rotation on its own axis. We see the same hemisphere illuminated. The other face is perpetually hidden from us.

During the winter of 1609, Galileo turned the first telescope on the Moon. He saw flat, vast, grey spaces, large and dark as oceans. He called them "seas".

On the 21st of July 1969 a space-module lands on the Sea of Tranquillity for the first time. Two men are aboard. Armstrong sets foot on the surface of the Moon, Aldrin jumps after him. In the cabin of the mother-ship *Apollo* 11 a third man, Collins, goes on turning round the Moon. They collect some grey dust and debris from the grey rocks covering the surface of the Moon. There are no colours, no gales sweeping the plains, no streams running down the mountains. No breeze blows ever. Not one living creature, not one insect; no meadows, no forests, no clouds, no echo.

The hunch-backed Moon has returned. Three-quarters through its course, the half-moon reappears with the play of light and shade alternating on its surface.

10–12. When night darkens, the shadow of the planet, hardly blurred, shows us the earth-shine. The crescent borders this zone of shadow. The light of Earth illumines the Moon.

13. A total eclipse of the Sun is an impressive sight. Daylight thins away. The solar crescent dwindles to a slim thread. Suddenly the Moon, hanging between the Sun and the Earth, hides the surface of the Sun exactly. A ghostly light covers the Earth. Around the Moon, a very bright ring. Then light returns.

14. Twelve new moons pass, a new year begins. The thin crescent comes back, 'the new moon with the old moon in her arm.'

45